BREATHING
UNDERWATER

SELECTED POEMS

BREATHING
UNDERWATER

SELECTED POEMS

Pablo Valdivia

Translated from the Spanish
By Ross Woods

With a Foreword
By Antonio Muñoz Molina

(A Spanish-English Bilingual Edition)

GUERNICA
TORONTO • BUFFALO • LANCASTER (U.K.)
2014

Original title: Respirar bajo el agua (2008): Editorial Alhulia
Copyright © 2008 by Pablo Valdivia and Editorial Alhulia
Translation copyright © 2014 Ross Woods and Guernica Editions Inc.

Michael Mirolla, editor
David Moratto, book designer
Guernica Editions Inc.
P.O. Box 76080, Abbey Market, Oakville, (ON), Canada L6M 3H5
2250 Military Road, Tonawanda, N.Y. 14150-6000 U.S.A.

Distributors:
University of Toronto Press Distribution,
5201 Dufferin Street, Toronto (ON), Canada M3H 5T8
Gazelle Book Services, White Cross Mills, High Town, Lancaster LA1 4XS U.K.

First edition.
Printed in Canada.

Legal Deposit – Third Quarter
Library of Congress Catalog Card Number: 2014934793
Library and Archives Canada Cataloguing in Publication

Valdivia, Pablo author
Breathing underwater : selected poems / Pablo Valdivia ; translated from the Spanish by Ross Woods ; with a foreword by Antonio Muñoz Molina. -- A Spanish-English bilingual edition.

(Essential translations series ; 22)
Translation of: Respirar bajo el agua.
Issued in print and electronic formats.
Text in English and Spanish.
ISBN 978-1-55071-879-9 (pbk.).--ISBN 978-1-55071-880-5 (epub).--
ISBN 978-1-55071-881-2 (mobi)

I. Woods, Ross, 1980-, translator II. Title. III. Series: Essential translations series ; 22

PQ6722.A44A2 2014   861'.7   C2014-900232-7   C2014-900233-5

CONTENTS ⟶

Londres y melancolía / London and Melancholy

Islas de noviembre / Islands of November

INTRODUCTION ———

Pablo Valdivia's debut collection, *Respirar bajo el agua* (*Breathing Underwater*), stands as a conversation between a young man and the world around him. It is a collection tinged with aching nostalgia—an emotion intensified by the often sterile images inspired by the Swedish and English backdrops in many of its poems. Fittingly, Valdivia borrows a line from Natalia Ginzburg to begin one section: "England is beautiful and melancholic." And, with this epigraph, he succinctly describes his own poems; they are beautiful and melancholic.

The following poem prefaces *Breathing Underwater*:

[THRESHOLD] ———

WE end up meeting so many times
in silence.

Words land like birds
on your shoulders when they observe Time.

Today I only want to look at you and November.

As well as placing the reader on the threshold of the collection, this poem signposts the book's central themes and tone. These five, image-laden lines are a powerful prologue to the verses that follow. Valdivia's constant dialogue with his surroundings is a predominant feature of the book. The despair and isolation he experiences when faced with harsh urban environments repeatedly offer stark contrast to the hope associated with the imagery of nature.

"[Threshold]" also exemplifies the poet's obsession with his own creative process, introducing a crucial motif: the written and spoken word. The imagery of words—the raw material that the poet must manipulate in order to produce his work—is fused here with the freedom of nature: "Words land like birds / on your shoulders when they observe Time." Frequently, the poet's focus on external factors imparts a timelessness to his verses. While these poems may seem ostensibly autobiographical in their subject matter, they also display an element of uncertainty that allows them to transcend the fixed moment which they seem to describe. This is evident here in the references to varied temporal expressions ("so many times," "Time," "November"). Indeed, one of Valdivia's preoccupations in *Breathing Underwater* is the desire to place the specific and the universal in opposition.

However, it is the title poem, "Breathing Underwater," which contains the collection's defining line: "Day has a pulse as difficult and strange / as breathing underwater." With these words, the poet expresses the figurative repercussions of an everyday, real-life experience. In this particular instance he describes how, when walking back to his dorm at the University of Nottingham in the middle of an English winter, the ferocity of the rain would make him feel as if the world itself had become submerged in water as he struggled to catch his breath. This most quotidian of tasks—returning home from work in the evening —thus becomes an almost impossible enterprise. The line acts as a metaphor for life in an increasingly anonymous society, where even the most mundane undertakings and harmless environments can make us feel as if we are attempting to breathe underwater, as if we are suffocating.

The thematic structure of *Breathing Underwater* rests on a continuous contrast between hope and pessimism. This is seen quite clearly at the end of the first section, with the clever juxtaposition of two of the finest poems in the book: "Breathing Underwater" and "Lights of Malmarna." Considered together, these poems stand out as a microcosmic representation of the dualities underpinning the narrative of this collection.

The intense melancholy of the title poem illustrates how the poet expresses his own feelings of solitude through a sense of enduring exile, as much physical as it is existential. This isolation is expressed in terms of the poet's surroundings: temporal/natural ("Spring"); man-made ("houses"); and social ("bodies" of people). Late in the day, during "the hopeless evenings," the poet finds some modicum of solace. However, this is a type of limbo, as evening does not amount to day or night. Indeed, neither day nor night offer respite. Night suffocates the poet, yet day is much the same. As we have seen, in the poem's outstanding line, life is as difficult as breathing underwater. The poem ends with an intense feeling of isolation, and the final lines imply that the poetic process only serves to compound the poet's loneliness.

Yet, almost immediately, "Lights of Malmarna," moves away from the haunting loneliness of "Breathing Underwater." Alone, one despairs; yet, with a partner, one is able to look to the future, to the "the vastness of a book / yet to be written". The snow is "muddy", the virgin innocence of its whiteness tarnished by dark marks, but this does not affect the poet. In fact, the strange lights offer a sense of newness which opens up a whole world of possibilities, later encapsulated by the image of the unwritten book. This poem reflects the hope inherent in Valdivia's poetry —a positivity that also helps the reader to look beyond the pessimism associated with modern life.

Though profoundly melancholic, *Breathing Underwater* is a collection of poetry filled with hope. In "Lights of Malmarna," the use of the verb "unveil" is linked to the "dawn," a recurrent image throughout the collection. There are many dawns in these poems, many possibilities for new beginnings, for new hope, as in the "daybreak" of "[The Valley]" or the "first light of winter" of "[Present]". The recollection of a deceased relative offers hope for the future in "[Memory of my Grandfather]": "Your memory and your voice / will rest with the dawn". The students of "Willoughby Hall," who seem drained by the monotony of university life, still have "the light of their eyes" and still retain hope "knowing / that tomorrow will be / snow, salt, grass, kisses."

Breathing Underwater works on the basic premise that without pessimism there can be no hope. This sentiment, so effectively expressed in the Spanish language, represented the most arduous challenge in the translation of the book into English. Indeed, aware that poetry itself, as Robert Frost put it, is what gets lost in translation, I have endeavoured to preserve as much as possible of the emotional power of the original poems. Ultimately, as Valdivia himself has noted, "Melancholy exists because hope exists and hope exists because negativity exists." This dichotomy serves to make *Breathing Underwater* a truly beautiful and melancholic collection of poems.

—*Ross Woods*

THE SOUL OF THE STRANGER ———
Antonio Muñoz Molina

Melancholy, clarity and plenitude are three characteristics present, to varying degrees, in each of the poems in this book. Read out of sequence—*jumping out of the bush*, as the metaphor goes in Spanish—they strike us as fragmentary glimpses of truths that we can all recognize, or as picture postcards of places that we recognize even though we have never been to them, even though we are never told their names. Melancholy and plenitude are visible in equal measure, often simultaneously. Yet, they are always expressed with a serenity uncommon in contemporary poetry, which itself is so prone—like almost all other art forms—to expressing indifference, to expressing pain, to using sarcasm to feign clarity. A sarcasm that in many cases is nothing more than heartlessness, or even worse, ethical and aesthetic overindulgence. In Pablo Valdivia's poems, sorrow can be very profound, but this never descends into mere posturing. Indeed, it makes me think of two famous Spanish poets: one who I know is important to him and whose influence is obvious, Antonio Machado; the other more remote and not well known outside the Spanish-speaking world but, nonetheless, fundamental to Valdivia's poetry, Fray Luis de León.

In Machado, and in Fray Luis, the great dramas of life are revealed to us more powerfully and more bitterly because their writing is always self-controlled. Self-controlled, literally, by the strict discipline imposed by rhyme and metre—which in their poetry always seems so uncluttered—and by a dignity reflected and accentuated by the clarity of their vocabulary. Pain and beauty exist simultaneously, alongside plenitude, alongside melancholy. The sense of loss is painful but it uncovers the value of the gift that makes its expression possible. Each poem in *Breathing Underwater* contains at least one drop of longing or desire, as well as another that celebrates life lived and life remembered. The passenger that we find lost on snowy northern plains, on the streets of rain-soaked cities, always retains at least a heartbeat, an ember of an indubitable sense of belonging, a loyalty to people and places dear to him, and a willingness to believe in hope. He would not be so alone and so lost if not for the warmth of the world in which he was raised and which he has left behind—and these poems never tell if he left by choice or necessity. And his loneliness never descends into nihilism or causes irreparable damage because of the hope of returns and reunions. Not all paradises are lost paradises, in spite of literature's indebtedness to them: Pablo Valdivia is one of those rare poets who has the honesty, or the bravery, or the sincerity, to speak of the satisfying sweetness of that tangible paradise that is love's gift.

The subtlety of this book's composition is best captured by reading it in fits and starts, through isolated encounters with each poem. This subtlety is always governed by an extreme economy of expression, which is the poetic reflection of that serenity or restraint that I referred to before. In these poems we find lots of verses of seven syllables and many of eleven, some rhythmically solemn alexandrines tempered by the colloquial nature of the language used, and very few rhymes, all of them assonant, in the style of Machado and another poet who is very present in the book (and in a dedication in the original Spanish version), Rafael Juárez.

But it is when the poems are read in the sequence chosen by the author that the flexibility of the book's plot becomes apparent. This plot unites them without subjecting them to the type of rigid structure that is detrimental to poetry like this. This book describes a consciousness in transit, a life on the move, a coming and going and a to-ing and fro-ing that encapsulates one of the most universal experiences of our time: nomadism and transience. Nomadism in space and time, because, here, geographical itineraries correspond to journeys from a past that at once remains very distant from an uncertain present as full of promises as it is of ambushes: journeys in time that are crueller because from them there is no return; journeys in which, above all, the baggage of the traveller consists of a list of what he has lost. But also of what most belongs to him, of a life lived and enjoyed, of that which is waiting for him: the hope of hearing a laugh, of once more experiencing "the dawn of happiness."

The collection's final line, "the soul of the stranger," perfectly plants the seed from which all the preceding verses have sprouted. But this also acts as a warning, as a sign, of all that is yet to come in the life and writing of Pablo Valdivia.

—*Translated by Ross Woods*

[LIMINAR] ⎯⎯

VENIMOS a encontrarnos tantas veces
en los silencios.

Las palabras se posan como un pájaro
en tus hombros cuando observan el tiempo.

Hoy sólo quiero mirarte y noviembre.

[THRESHOLD] ———

WE end up meeting so many times
in silence.

Words land like birds
on your shoulders when they observe Time.

Today I only want to look at you and November.

Luces de Malmarna / Lights of Malmarna

———

Skuggor skrider genom mina riken,
slocknade ljusgestalter.
Shadows glide through my lands,
quenched shapes of light.

— PÄR LAGERKVIST

MALMARNA ⸺

Malmarna, cuánto escondes
e iluminas trillando el aire nuevo.

En tu océano lanza mi voz lastre
y despliega sus alas
de silencio tocando el horizonte.

Dime, bajo qué luces
aguardan las palabras verdaderas
que aliviarán de nieve la mirada.

Malmarna ——

Malmarna, you hide and uncover
so much, threshing the new air.

My voice throws ballast into your ocean
and spreads its silent
wings, touching the horizon.

Tell me, under which lights
are they waiting, the words of truth
that clear the snow from my vision.

CULPA ———

Contemplo lo que queda de nosotros
sobre la nieve,
las palabras que abaten nuestros pasos
y los hunden con sus voces oscuras.

Los puentes arden. Noche sobre el lago.
Se abre el espejismo helado del agua:
la cárcel silenciosa de la aurora.

La culpa tiene colores extraños
y palpita en los aromas del frío.

BLAME ——

I contemplate what remains of us
upon the snow,
the words which erase our footprints
and sink them with their dark sounds.

The bridges are burning. Night on the lake.
The frozen illusion of the water opens up:
the silent prison of dawn.

Blame is tinged with strange colours
and pulsates in the aromas of the cold.

PORVENIR ———

La luz rema con fuerza
sin dirección.
Nuestra carne parece que es de otros, de cualquiera
que nunca conocimos.

Te alejas de la orilla
y desde el fondo
restos de nubes
reclaman tu semblante.

En el lecho del agua
el porvenir nos espera sentado
sobre un banco de ilusión sumergida.

FUTURE ———

The light rows strongly
without direction.
Our flesh seems of others, of somebody
we never knew.

You move away from the shore
and from the background
the remains of clouds
summon your expression.

On the bed of the lake
the future awaits us sitting
upon a sandbank of submerged hope.

PUERTAS ———

Sangra la condena de nuestra puerta,
porque ya no la cruzarán más llaves
ni más sonrisas.

La estancia espera con la cerradura
dormida hasta que una voz la despierte.

Los días se suceden,
mientras algunas puertas
ahogan de óxido sus bisagras
y otras encierran nuestras ilusiones.

Cuando supuren ruina los umbrales
quizá la alegría regrese, siempre
tan lejana, siempre tan inconstante.

Doors ———

Condemnation bleeds from our door
because no more keys
or smiles will cross it now.

The room waits, its keyhole
dormant, until a voice awakens it.

Days pass by,
while some doors
drown their hinges with rust
and others lock in our hopes.

When the thresholds ooze ruin
perhaps happiness will return, always
so far away, always so fickle.

RECUERDO ——

En tu voz no resuellan las auroras
sino los pasos huecos de la noche.
Has vertido tus anclas en los árboles,
pero hay pesos que habitan en la piel
y reabren heridas.

Buscas una madrugada, recuerdo,
donde yacer sereno
al abrazo vivo de arroyos libres
de angustia y de sombra.

Ten paciencia que el tiempo
dejará limpio el cauce
de la desdicha
y con su luz sanará el dolor
donde aún se estremece tu esperanza.

Recollection ───

Your voice exhales not the day's dawning
but the hollow footsteps of the night.
You have dropped anchor on the trees,
but there is a heaviness which lives in the skin
and reopens wounds.

You search for a daybreak, I remember,
where the vivid embrace
of streams free of anguish and
shadow rests calmly.

Have patience that time
will leave the path
of misfortune clear
and with its light it will cure the pain
where your hopes still tremble.

LAS BAÑISTAS ———

Las bañistas nadan entre las horas
mientras sus pies impulsan
el tiempo hacia el borde de la piscina.

Bajo el agua dormida se besan poco a poco
y con sus labios vierten
burbujas de alegría
que el aire desvanece.

Quisiera hundirme
cerca de su esperanza para siempre,
que el dolor por fin flote
lejos de mi sonrisa.

The Swimmers

The swimmers swim for hours
while their legs propel
time towards the edge of the pool.

Beneath the sleeping water they kiss gently
and from their lips they pour
bubbles of happiness
that the air disperses.

I would like to submerge myself
near their hope forever,
so that pain would finally float
away from my smile.

RESPIRAR BAJO EL AGUA —

Me sumerjo en las tardes
sin esperanza
de los primeros días
de primavera.

La luz es un sonido
de cuerpos que caminan a lo lejos,
de ilusiones que viven en las casas.

La noche empieza
a asfixiarme sin pausa.

El día tiene un pulso tan difícil y extraño
como respirar bajo el agua. Frío.
Mientras tanto la soledad escribe
mi nombre por el aire.

BREATHING UNDERWATER

I submerge myself in the
hopeless evenings
of the first days
of Spring.

Light is a sound
of bodies that walk in the distance,
of illusions that live in houses.

Night begins
to suffocate me relentlessly.

Day has a pulse as difficult and strange
as breathing underwater. Cold.
Meanwhile loneliness writes
my name in the air.

LUCES DE MALMARNA ⎯⎯

Son extrañas las luces de Malmarna
cuando su tacto débil nos sorprende
caminando sobre la nieve turbia.

Tenemos la sensación de que todo
es nuevo, que cada día inaugura
su forma con nosotros.

Estas islas, esta latitud blanca
sin cielo, alumbran
todas nuestras promesas.

Nos miramos. La vastedad de un libro
por escribir.

La verdad de este aquí, ahora, siempre.

LIGHTS OF MALMARNA ⟋

The lights of Malmarna are strange
when their faint touch surprises us
walking on the muddy snow.

We have the feeling that everything
is new, that each day unveils
its form to us.

These islands, this white, skyless
latitude, illuminate
all our promises.

We look at each other. The vastness of a book
yet to be written.

The truth of this here, now, always.

Lindes sin tiempo / Timeless Boundaries

————

Estos campos, inmensa sinfonía en sangre reseca ...
These fields, immense symphony in dried-up blood ...

— FEDERICO GARCÍA LORCA

[EL VALLE] ———

Por fin has regresado
al seno de los fardos,
a las piquetas vivas
de los amaneceres.
De los olivos cuelgan
ojos negros de invierno
que estallan de alegría
junto a las almazaras.
Festejan tu mirada
feliz, despierta, limpia.
El valle ya susurra
tu nombre verdadero.

[THE VALLEY] ———

Finally you have returned
to the bosom of the olive piles,
to the lively pickaxes
of daybreak.
Hanging from the olive trees
are black wintry eyes
that burst with happiness
beside the mills.
They celebrate your face:
happy, alert, clean.
The valley is already whispering
your true name.

[PECHO COLORADO] ⸺

Merienda en los olivos.
Las piquetas sostienen
los troncos y las cribas
descansan aceituna.
Se fragua tu destino
entre aquellos hermanos.
Imágenes que vuelven
de tu pasado. Roja
tierra por la pendiente
que ya nadie cultiva.
En ella hablan tus sueños,
de ella bebe tu vida.

[RED CHEST] ⟶

Picnic amongst the olive trees.
The pickaxes support
the logs and the sieves
offer respite to the olives.
Your destiny is forged
between these brothers.
Images that return
from your past. On
the slope, red earth
that nobody tills anymore.
In it your dreams speak,
from it your life drinks.

[TODO VUELVE] ———

El camino murió
al crepúsculo ciego
del invierno intranquilo.
Rugía fuerte el viento
en los portones secos
donde ya no conversan
la luz y los ancianos.
Se alejan con las horas
nuestras voces y el año.
Todo vuelve y se agota.

[EVERYTHING RETURNS] ⸻

The path died
at the blind twilight
of the restless winter.
The wind howled violently
in the dry doorways
where the light and the elderly
no longer converse.
Our voices and the year
distance themselves as the hours pass.
Everything returns and perishes.

[UN FAMILIAR] ———

En noches de aceituna
cruza aún por las sendas
desdichadas al raso
de estraperlo y de sangre.
Ahora admira el brío
de las estacas vivas.
Muerto y solemne escucha
reverdecer olivos.
La tierra entre sus manos
es un hilo de nombres.

[A RELATIVE] ⸺

On olive-scented nights
he still crosses ill-fated
paths into the open country
of the black market and blood.
Now he admires the verve
of the vivid stakes.
Dead and solemn, he listens
to the olive trees turn green.
The earth in his hands
is a thread of names.

[S U E Ñ O] ———

Suenan cascos de un mulo,
vienen lejos, de un sueño,
de la niebla profunda
que duerme en el helado
semblante de los muertos
y de nuestra memoria.
Frontera de la noche
y mis antepasados.
Bajo el balcón los hombres
varean las estrellas.

[DREAM] ——

The hooves of a mule sound,
they come from afar, from a dream,
from the deep mist
that sleeps in the frozen
face of the dead
and of our memory.
Border of the night
and my ancestors.
Under the balcony the men
thresh the stars.

[PALABRAS] ———

Cuando hablamos el tiempo
se distancia y escucho
el balanceo vivo
de mi edad en sus ojos.
Hoy conversamos mientras
se consumen alegres
hojas de olivo y tarde.
Remanso de palabras,
diálogos de la lumbre.

[WORDS] ⸺

When we talk time
distances itself and I hear
the living to-and-fro
of my age in your eyes.
Today we chat while
happy olive leaves
and evening waste away.
Haven of words,
dialogues of firelight.

[PRESENTE] ——

Primera luz de invierno,
memoria en las pupilas.
Caen las hojas lejos
y tu mirada pulcra
recuerda aquella casa,
viejos nombres, un beso.
El pasado alimenta
el trigo del presente.

[PRESENT] ———

First light of Winter,
memory in the pupils.
The leaves fall far
and your immaculate face
recalls that house,
old names, a kiss.
The past nurtures
the wheat of the present.

[Diciembre] ⸺

Mediodía de invierno,
caminos silenciosos
por donde la luz tiembla.
El agua de diciembre
es voz que se levanta
por la acequia a tus ojos.
Sois el mismo. Piel, agua,
cuerpos que asola el tiempo.

[December] ———

Midday in Winter,
silent paths
along which the light trembles.
December's water
is sound that raises itself
up the ditch to your eyes.
You are both the same. Skin, water,
bodies that devastate time.

[PLAZA] ———

Desmorona la plaza
el viento. Los recuerdos
descansan como escombros
rendidos, invisibles,
bajo nuestros zapatos.
Camino sin mirarte.
El otoño sacude
esta amistad tramposa.
Deja que arrastren todo
el dolor tus palabras.

[SQUARE] ———

The wind destroys
the square. Memories
are buried like exhausted
debris, invisible,
under our shoes.
I walk without looking at you.
Autumn shakes
this false friendship.
Let your words drag
all the pain along with them.

[*RECUERDO DE MI ABUELO*] ⎯⎯

No bailará la luz
en tu regazo. Triste
perseguirá tu gorra
el rastro de la tierra.
Yacerán con la aurora
tu recuerdo y tu voz.
Tu sombra buscará
el rumor del olivo.
Silencio por tu nombre.
Silencio por el viento.

[MEMORY OF MY GRANDFATHER] ——

The light will no longer dance
on your lap. Sadly
your cap will pursue
the sandy trail.
Your memory and your voice
will rest with the dawn.
Your shadow will search for
the murmur of the olive tree.
Silence for your name.
Silence on the wind.

Londres y melancolía / London and Melancholy

Inglaterra es hermosa y melancólica.
England is beautiful and melancholic.

— NATALIA GINZBURG

CIUDAD INSOMNE ——

Londres se está muriendo
de la melancolía
que palpita en sus huesos.

Aquí el tiempo pasó y dejó condenada
la ciudad a un momento
decrépito y sombrío anterior a la Historia,
que se vierte en silencio.

Las mejillas insomnes
de las casas ficticias en que habitan fantasmas
y hombres alucinados,
se quiebran con el roce del agua de la lluvia
y se van derrumbando poco a poco por dentro.

En la luz de la tarde,
se hunde ya lentamente la mirada en el cieno.

Sleepless City

London is dying
from the melancholy
that beats in its bones.

Here time has passed and has left the city
condemned to a decrepit
and dismal moment prior to History,
which spills itself into silence.

The sleepless cheeks
of the fictitious houses where ghosts and
stunned men live
crack with the touch of the rainwater
and inside they collapse little by little.

In the evening light,
the gaze slowly sinks into the mud.

WILLOUGHBY HALL ——

Llegan a Willoughby los estudiantes
con el hábito triste
del cansancio y el frío.

En el camino hay nieve,
hay sal y algunos besos prendidos en el hielo
de la hierba y de los días.

Caminan sin saber
que mañana serán
nieve, sal, hierba, besos.

El invierno ha clavado su sonrisa de sombra
en la luz de sus ojos.

WILLOUGHBY HALL ⟍

The students arrive at Willoughby
with the sad habit
of tiredness and the cold.

There is snow on the path,
there is salt and some kisses snatched in the ice
of the grass and the days.

They walk without knowing
that tomorrow will be
snow, salt, grass, kisses.

Winter has nailed its shadowy smile
to the light of their eyes.

RELOJES ———

Hoy por la mañana estaban nublados
los relojes. Ya no se distinguía
ni el temblor del segundero
ni el calor de su esperanza.

Blancas quejas infinitas
hilaban el porvenir.

CLOCKS ⎯⎯

Today, in the morning, the clocks
were cloudy. One could no longer distinguish
the trembling of the small hand
nor the heat of its hope.

Infinite white protests
spin the future.

Río ——

A veces en las tardes
el río evoca el ruido
alejado del mar
a través de las hojas del castaño;
con su ruido regresan
miradas tan escuálidas
como nubes de estío.

Esas miradas luchan
contra el curso del agua,
intentan escalar
de chilanco a chilanco
para asaltar el tiempo
y vencer la nostalgia.

Son como mis recuerdos,
ilusiones que doma la corriente.

River —

Sometimes in the evenings
the river evokes the distant
noise of the sea
through the leaves of the chestnut tree;
with its noise faces
as thin as the clouds
of summer return.

These faces fight
against the course of the water,
they try to climb
from pool to pool
to attack time
and defeat nostalgia.

They are like my memories,
illusions that tame the current.

SOLEDAD ———

Muere lluvia tranquila
de los atardeceres
en la piel de los niños.

Juegan cerca del lago
mientras un velo lento
los envuelve con calma
hasta que se evaporan
en la luz densa y triste.

Soledad era esto.
El frío del silencio
murmurando en los huesos,
la prisión infinita
de la que nadie escapa.

Loneliness ———

Nightfall's peaceful
rain dies
on the skin of children.

They play near the lake
while a slow kite
envelops them with calm
until they evaporate
in the dense and sad light.

This was loneliness.
The coldness of silence
whispering in the bones,
the infinite prison
from which none escape.

BARCA ———

En los atardeceres
anónimos y lentos,
en los puentes dormidos por la niebla,
Londres se acerca calma
a susurrar tu nombre.

Nadie sabe de quién son estos pasos,
si los sigues, si arrastran
tu cuerpo a la deriva
entre riberas, frágil
como barca de invierno.

Boat

In the anonymous
and slow evenings,
on the bridges put to sleep by fog,
London calmly comes
to whisper your name.

Nobody knows who owns these footsteps,
if you follow them, if they drag
your body adrift
between banks, fragile
like a winter boat.

SOHO ———

Tus mejillas descansan
en un charco del Soho.

Las calles te recuerdan
el sur, el beso último.

No hay regreso posible.
Tus ojos surcan aguas
negras de olvido y lodo.

En tu rostro lejano,
el tiempo ya camina
sin pulso.

SOHO ——

Your cheeks rest
in a Soho puddle.

The streets remind you
of the south, the last kiss.

There is no possible return.
Your eyes cross black
waters of forgetfulness and mud.

In your distant face,
time already walks
without a pulse.

BOSQUES ———

Hay bosques a lo lejos
donde las hojas son Londres y la mañana.

Camino hacia esos árboles
para perder mi luz por sus senderos.

Quiero olvidar la aurora
y recobrar la noche, la sombra, tu recuerdo.

Woods ⸺

There are distant woods
where the leaves are London and the morning.

I walk towards those trees
to lose my light on their paths.

I want to forget the dawn
and recover the night, the shadow, your memory.

CERRAR LOS OJOS ⎯⎯

Londres cierra sus ojos
de bruma y calles muertas.
Se condena al olvido,
soporta que los pasos indiferentes, rostros,
siluetas fantasmales, derroten sus aceras
en los días de plomo.

Algunas veces Londres y yo somos el mismo.
Cierro mis ojos yermos y le ruego a la gente
que me bese pausada con la luz del desprecio.

Es demasiado fácil darle la espalda al mundo;
por eso aún te busco, entre las multitudes
que quiebran la esperanza.

No permita tu cuerpo
que venza la mañana.
Cuando por fin te encuentre, que tu piel me haga súbdito
del asombro y el viento.

CLOSE YOUR EYES ───

London closes its eyes,
misty and filled with dead streets.
It is damned to suffer oblivion,
it allows indifferent footsteps, faces,
ghostly silhouettes, to destroy its footpaths
in days of lead.

Sometimes London and I are the same.
I close my barren eyes and ask people
to kiss me slowly with the light of disdain.

It is too easy to turn your back on the world;
because of this I still look for you, among the crowds
that destroy hope.

Do not allow your body
to defeat tomorrow.
When I finally find you, let your skin make me subject
to amazement and wind.

ADIÓS LONDRES ───

Londres desde los cielos es una flor nevada
que no termina nunca.
El invierno ha colmado
la sombra de mis ojos con su nostalgia viva
y el eco anaranjado de los techos helados,
para que así recuerde
cómo en Londres un beso, en alguna avenida,
agota su rumor y quiebra mi esperanza.

Londres es la metáfora de un río
sin salida,
la ficción de un amor
que se duerme en la tarde.

Goodbye London ⎯⎯

London from the skies is a snowy flower
that never ends.
The winter has stretched the shadow
of my eyes to their limits with its living nostalgia
and the orangey echo of the icy roofs,
so that in this way I remember
how in London a kiss, in some avenue,
exhausts its murmur and breaks my hope.

London is the metaphor for a river
with no exit,
the fiction of a love
that sleeps in the afternoon.

Islas de noviembre / Islands of November

———

Vio de oro, de mármol y de sol amable
la ciudad de silencio, de amor y de crepúsculo.
He saw it golden, of marble and of friendly sun
the city of silence, of love and twilight.

— RUBÉN DARÍO

Noche de otoño,
la voz del viento.
Lluvia de ahora,
nuestros recuerdos.

Otoño y risas
luz de hoy en que te espero.

Autumn night,
the voice of the wind.
Rain of now,
our memories.

Autumn and laughter
today's light in which I await you.

Ceniza y pena
vienen de lejos.

Miro atrás y contemplo
lo que ya he sido,
lo que seré,
lo que no ha muerto.

Ash and sorrow
come from afar.

I look back and contemplate,
what I have been,
what I will be,
what has not died.

¿Quién sentó a la mesa esta luz calma?

Almorzamos silencio,
tejas y claroscuros.

Who sat this calm light on the table?

We lunch on silence,
tiles and chiaroscuros.

Aprender en los días
lo que no cambia,
lo que se mueve.

Levantarse sin miedo
a perderse solo por los canales.

Hojas antiguas
son los recuerdos
que caminan sonriendo los castaños.

Mientras todo es rehacerse, volver
a escribir en las horas,
ensayar a dormir
tranquilo entre tus brazos.

To learn in the days
what does not change,
what moves.

To arise without fear of
losing oneself among the channels.

Ancient leaves
are the memories
that walk smiling at the chestnuts.

While everything is to reconstruct oneself, to write
again in the hours,
to practice sleeping
peacefully in your arms.

¿Qué aguarda cuando nos separamos?

Esquinas romas,
cuerpos donde las horas apelmazan
un sabor raro a deseo y memoria.

Ilusión por vivir el reencuentro,
besos borrando
latitudes exactas
y meridianos firmes.

Luces grises y espera.

What awaits when we separate?

Blunt corners,
bodies where the hours make
a strange flavor of desire and memory cling.

Hopes of living the reunion,
kisses erasing
exact latitudes,
steady meridians.

Grey lights and waiting.

A veces en la tarde soñolienta
me veo lento, solo,
dentro de un cuadro inconcluso. Luz yerma.
Mis bolsillos monótonos
guardan aire, quimeras de tu nombre,
caminos sin tu rostro.

Sometimes in the sleepy afternoon
I see myself slow, alone,
in an unfinished painting. Barren light.
My monotonous pockets
hold air, chimeras of your name,
paths without your face.

El agua tiene una puerta
que abren los recuerdos vivos.
Tu cuerpo es su llave maestra.

⁓

Volverá con la marea.
La muerte, como las algas,
enredará lo que anhelas.

⁓

El horizonte es tu cuerpo
que atardece. Su luz
es tu nombre: voz del tiempo.

Water has a door
that opens living memories.
Your body is its master key.

—

It will return with the tide.
Death, like seaweed,
entangles what you desire.

—

The horizon is your body
which darkens. Its light
is your name: voice of time.

Palabras en una tarde
de levante y viento:
mentiras, ojos de amantes.

⁓

En el eco de los días
cabalga mi voz tus sueños.
Nuestra esperanza tu risa.

⁓

Arena y palabras, viento.
La aurora de la alegría
muerde tu sombra y los besos.

Words on an afternoon
of *levante* and wind:
lies, eyes of lovers.

—

In the echo of days
my voice straddles your dreams.
Our hope your laugh.

—

Sand and words, wind.
The dawn of happiness
bites your shadow and the kisses.

La sombra desnuda aguarda
a otra sombra que no llega.
La espera es una flor agria.

—

Como en una despedida,
el sol lo arrasará todo.
Qué noche tan fugitiva.

—

Mirar rasgando un espejo
y no ver más que palabras:
el alma del extranjero.

The naked shadow waits
for another shadow that doesn't arrive.
Waiting is a bitter flower.

—

As in a farewell,
the sun destroys everything.
What a fugitive night.

—

To look scratching a mirror
and to see nothing but words:
the soul of the stranger.

ACKNOWLEDGEMENTS ────

My thanks go to the author, Pablo Valdivia, for his friendship and assistance while fine-tuning these English versions of his poetry. Thanks are also due to Antonio Muñoz Molina, who graciously agreed to write a foreword to this selection of translations, and to Valdivia's Spanish Publishers, Editorial Alhulia, for the permission to publish the original versions of the poems. Furthermore, I would like to acknowledge the Faculty of Humanities and Social Sciences, Victoria University of Wellington, New Zealand for a Research Grant that facilitated the publication of this book. Finally, I am indebted to Sarah Woods, Marco Sonzogni and Hamish Clayton for their constant support and advice.

ABOUT THE AUTHOR ——

Pablo Valdivia is Assistant Professor in Spanish Literature at the University of Amsterdam, The Netherlands. His poetry has been published in Spain over the course of the last decade, initially in Spanish literary magazines such as *Letra Clara* and *Imaginando*, as well as the national newspaper *El País*. In 2004, a selection of seven poems was included in an anthology of young Andalusian poets, *Poesía por venir* (*Poetry to Come*), published by Editorial Renacimiento. Valdivia's first collection of poetry, *Respirar bajo el agua* (*Breathing Underwater*), was published in 2008 by Editorial Alhulia. His second collection, *La velocidad de la niebla* (*The Speed of Mist*), appeared in late 2011. In addition to his poetic output Valdivia has published critical work on Federico García Lorca, including the book *La vereda indecisa: El viaje hacia la literatura de Federico García Lorca* (Granada: Diputación de Granada, 2010). His latest work is a critical edition of the novel *Sefarad* by the award-winning Spanish author Antonio Muñoz Molina.

Ross Woods' academic research focuses on the work of the Spanish poet José Manuel Caballero Bonald. He is the author of numerous articles on Bonald as well as the book, *Understanding the Poetry of José Manuel Caballero Bonald: The Function of Memory in a Spanish Writer's Art*. Woods' translation of Italian poet Eugenio Montale's poem, "In the Smoke," appeared in *Corno inglese*, an anthology of Montale's poetry in English translation, edited by Marco Sonzogni.

Printed in June 2014
by Gauvin Press,
Gatineau, Québec